SISTER TERESA

Written by Amy Heebner

SISTER TERESA

INT. CHAPEL, CONVENT IN AVILA, 1561.

Nuns are gathered for noontime prayer in the chapel. They sing a hymn, then close their eyes and begin saying the Pater Noster (Lord's Prayer) in Latin.

TERESA, a beautiful nun in her 40s, rises above the ground, eyes closed in prayer, a blissful expression on her face.

She hovers, floating in place, while the prayer continues.

On either side of her, the nuns -- including Sister BEATRICE on one side -- gaze at TERESA, admiring her piety.

TERESA gently comes back to earth. The praying aloud stops. Sister HELEN moves to the pulpit and opens the Bible. She reads aloud in Latin (Matthew 13: 3-4.)

SUBTITLES:

"The Parable of the Sower. Behold, a sower went forth to sow; and when he sowed, some seeds fell by the wayside, and the fowls came and devoured them up: Some fell upon stony places, where they had not much earth: and forthwith they sprung up, because they had no deepness of earth: And when the sun was up, they were scorched; and because they had no root, they withered away."

INT. HALLWAY - CONVENT.

Nuns are filing out of the chapel after noontime
worship. Sister Teresa hurries in the opposite
direction, carrying a Bible.

                    HELEN

          Sister Teresa, where are you going?

                    TERESA

          I'm preparing for a meeting, Sister Helen.

Sister Beatrice walks with Sister Teresa.

                    BEATRICE

          Are you going forward with the meeting for
     the villagers?

                    TERESA

          Yes.

                    BEATRICE

          What if they don't come?

                    TERESA

          They're coming! A group is waiting in the
     yard!

                    BEATRICE

          I will help you.

                    TERESA

          Very good! We'll need to bring some
     chairs.

EXT. YARD OUTSIDE CONVENT IN AVILA. A FEW MINUTES
LATER.

Teresa and Beatrice each carry chairs, which they
place in the yard. The villagers are waiting, some
seated on benches.

                    BEATRICE

          This is quite a group!

                    TERESA

          Welcome to the convent yard!

                    LOPE

          Sister, what is this meeting about?

                    TERESA

          The constable brought us ten people to
          chastise last week. We'd like to hear your side
          of the story.

                    ELSA

          Who did you chastise?

                    PABLO

          What were they accused of?

                    BEATRICE

          We cannot tell you the names of the
          persons. That's confidential. Each one
          confessed their sins and received forgiveness.

                    TERESA

          Husband and wife were arguing bitterly in
          every instance.

                    LADY GONZALEZ

          What kind of domestic dispute?

TERESA

Several men were going to a tavern instead of going home after working in the fields. Their wives were upset.

CARLOS

Maybe they found better company at the tavern!

TERESA

Maybe you're right. That's why we asked to talk with the wives too.

BEATRICE

One man was caught stealing food. He was trying to satisfy his wife, who wanted him to bring home more money to buy food.

PABLO

What about the others?

TERESA

One was a woman, caught whipping a cart horse almost to death. The horse got stuck with the cart in mud. The woman was so angry that she beat the horse mercilessly! She was angry about many things, not just the cart stuck in the mud.

ELSA

I understand. Some days it seems that nothing goes right. A plate breaks, the soup boils over, the children fight with each other ...

MARITZA

... rain falls on the laundry drying on the line...

                    ELSA

     At night when my husband comes home,
sometimes I am too tired to make him feel
special.

                   TERESA

At least you try to make him feel special.

                    ELSA

Yes, I try.

                    LOPE

     I wish the woman who whipped the cart
horse were here. She might learn something from
what you say.

                   TERESA

     That is one purpose of these meetings, to
learn from each other. What other problems would
you like to discuss?

                  MARITZA

     My husband often goes to the tavern at
night. I wish he would stay home.

                   CARLOS

What do you do at night when he is there?

                  MARITZA

     There is so much to do! Cleaning up after
dinner, repairing whatever is broken ...

                   CARLOS

     That is work! He probably goes to the
tavern to escape working for you at home!

                   TERESA

     Your husband works a full day in the
fields.   What do others do at night?

                                              4

                    LOPE

     My wife and I play cards. It passes the
time.

                    ELSA

     We tell stories to the children and to
each other.

               LADY GONZALEZA

     I like it when my husband talks about his
day at work, about the people he's met.

                  BEATRICE

     These are all ways to be a good companion
for your husband.

                  MARITZA

     What about me? Don't I get any time off?
Maybe I should go to the tavern!

                  TERESA

     You   could   enjoy   your   husband's
companionship at night.

                   PAULO

     Doesn't anybody play with their wife at
night?

                  CARLOS

You mean sex?

                   PAULO

Yes, I mean sex play.

                  CARLOS

My wife doesn't want another child yet.

               LADY GONZALEZ

     There are things you can do that don't
make babies.

                          CARLOS

              Tell that to my wife!

Some of the villagers laugh.

                          TERESA

              So this is a situation other couples have
         experienced. Each villager nods their head or
         says "Yes."

                          TERESA

         What can we do to help?

                          ELSA

              This meeting is good. It's good to hear
         what other people are thinking. If we could have
         more meetings . . . .

                          TERESA

              Would you like to have a weekly meeting
         here at the convent?

The villagers agree, nodding and commenting.

                          LOPE

              I will tell my neighbors.

                          ELSA

              So will I. Maybe we will have peace in my
         neighborhood at last -- if people come to the
         meetings.

INT. TERESA'S ROOM AT THE CONVENT. SEVERAL WEEKS
LATER. AFTERNOON.

Teresa is writing in her journal at a small table.
She reads aloud what she has written.

                    TERESA

     "We had another lively meeting with the
villagers! People speak frankly about their
problems at home. I think this is good."

A knock at the door. Teresa finds Sister Jana and
Sister Beatrice waiting at the door.

                    JANA

     Sister Teresa?

                    TERESA

     Yes, Sister Jana?

                    JANA

     This letter came for you, from the
Inquisition in Madrid. It must be important.
Are you in trouble?

                    TERESA

     I certainly hope not.

Teresa accepts the letter. Sister Beatrice looks on
with kind concern.

                    JANA

     Who were you talking to?

                    TERESA

     I was reading aloud from my journal. My
confessor told me to write regularly in my
journal.

                    JANA

     You're lucky, Teresa! I wish I had
permission to write.

Sister Jana walks away.

                         BEATRICE

          What is in the letter, Teresa?

                          TERESA

          You read it, please.

Beatrice opens the letter and reads it silently.

                         BEATRICE

          It says you must go to the Cathedral in
          Madrid to talk with one of the Inquisitors.

                          TERESA

          Does it say why?

Beatrice scans the document, then passes it to
Teresa.

                         BEATRICE

          No explanation at all.

                          TERESA

          I have met the Inquisitor before -- Father
          Ruiz. He let me go without chastising me.

                         BEATRICE

          Maybe it is good news!

                          TERESA

          Maybe. Maybe word has reached him of the
          meetings with the villagers. I did not ask
          permission from Madrid.

                         BEATRICE

          You should have asked permission first.

                          TERESA

          They might have said "no!"

                    TERESA (CONT'D)

     The constable wishes we would chastise the
troublesome villagers. But we give confession
first.

                    BEATRICE

     Surely the Inquisitors will not quarrel
with giving confession!

                    TERESA

     I hope not. Thanks, Beatrice, for your
support. The trip takes two days. I must get
ready.

                    BEATRICE

     Let me know if I can help.

INT. CATHEDRAL IN MADRID. ONE WEEK LATER. AFTERNOON.

Sister Teresa enters through the large door at the
back of the sanctuary. Sunlight floods the entrance.
She genuflects, then walks to the altar where FATHER
RUIZ is waiting.

                    FATHER RUIZ

     Sister Teresa, do you know why we summoned
you here?

                    TERESA

     No, Father Ruiz.

                    FATHER RUIZ

     (with resignation in his voice)

     Would you like to guess?

                    TERESA

     No, thank you. Please tell me in what way
I have erred.

                    FATHER RUIZ

You are teaching lifestyle, Teresa.

                      TERESA

We teach the value of daily prayer, of
reading the Holy Gospel, attending
service, the confession of sins. In what
way are these teachings offensive, Holy
Father?

                    FATHER RUIZ

We are told you teach "sex education."

                      TERESA

(genuinely shocked) I beg your pardon?

                    FATHER RUIZ

(ominously) What did you say?

                      TERESA

With respect, I must ask where this
information came from.

                    FATHER RUIZ

Our sources are not your concern.

                      TERESA

Father, I have not used the term "sex
education" even once!

                    FATHER RUIZ

I am told the villagers use the term quite
freely!

                      TERESA

The villagers?! You refer to our meetings
with the villagers to discuss their problems.

                    FATHER RUIZ

          Meetings with the villagers?

                      TERESA

          The village constable brings citizens to
     us for chastising when they are found to be in
     error.

                    FATHER RUIZ

          Do you chastise them?

                      TERESA

          First we offer confession, then we discuss
     the problem at hand. This led to regular weekly
     meetings.

                    FATHER RUIZ

          What do you do at these meetings?

                      TERESA

          We lead discussions. We talk about what
     the Holy Bible teaches us about marriage and
     child-rearing in a Christian context.

                    FATHER RUIZ

          Do you discuss sex?

                      TERESA

          If the parishioners want to discuss sex,
     then we discuss sex -- respectfully and with an
     eye to what our Lord has taught us.

                    FATHER RUIZ

          Teaching about sex has not been sanctioned
     by the Church. When we asked you to teach, we
     assumed you would teach the other nuns. Instead
     you are teaching the parishioners directly.

TERESA

You are correct. I teach the nuns and the villagers together, in our meetings about family values.

FATHER RUIZ

What about your writing, Teresa?

TERESA

Yes?

FATHER RUIZ

You were instructed to write about your experiences. Have you had any other mystical experiences?

TERESA

Nothing unusual since our last conversation. Just the intense happiness during devotional prayer. And sometimes the floating above the ground, for a short time. As you instructed, I write regularly in my diary.

FATHER RUIZ

Every day?

TERESA

I try to write at least every two days or so, mostly about our daily life at the convent and the meetings with the villagers.

FATHER RUIZ

Good.

TERESA

Father, if you could only meet the couples and families who come to our meetings!

FATHER RUIZ

If I could meet them?

                         TERESA

     You would see for yourself how they yearn
to understand the mysteries of love, human love
and divine love. After our meetings, people go
home with a new attitude, respecting each other.
In the past many of the same people spent the
evenings in taverns instead of at home.

                       FATHER RUIZ

     How many?

                         TERESA

     About forty people attended our last
meeting.

                       FATHER RUIZ

     (impressed) Forty people!

                         TERESA

     Now the taverns are often peaceful. We
hear conversation and music in the village at
night, where we formerly observed drunken
fights and vandalism.

                     TERESA (CONT'D)

     Some of the villagers have written letters
to me. May I read one to you?

                       FATHER RUIZ

     Yes.

She draws from her satchel a small stack of letters
carefully tied with a string. Teresa opens the first
letter in the stack.

                              TERESA

                        (reading aloud)

        Dear   Sister   Teresa,   Your   afternoon
    meetings have made a beautiful difference in
    our family.

                         (MORE)

                    TERESA (CONT'D)

        My husband comes home now after working in
    the fields instead of spending his evenings at
    the tavern.

INT. ELSA'S HOME. EVENING.

An evening scene by candlelight at Elsa's home, with
Teresa's voice reading the letter in voice-over. The
children clear the dinner table. Elsa's husband sits
at table and talks to Elsa. A daughter sits at a
table writing a letter.

                      TERESA (V.O.)

        The children help with household duties,
    often before I have to ask them. I can send you
    this letter because my daughter has learned to
    write at your convent school. She writes letters
    for the neighbors too, and they pay her a coin.
    Maybe when she grows up my daughter will become
    a scribe in our village! We are grateful to you
    for helping us understand how to respect and
    love each other.

INT. CATHEDRAL IN MADRID. CONTINUOUS.

                     FATHER RUIZ

        This is a gratifying letter, Teresa. Are
    the others like this one?

Teresa offers him the small stack of letters. He
accepts them.

                         TERESA

        The   other   letters   also   praise   our
meetings.

                      FATHER RUIZ

        So you have had some success.

                         TERESA

        There is more harmony among the couples in
the village. The constable has brought us fewer
people to chastise.

                      FATHER RUIZ

        All right. You may continue your meetings
with the villagers, as long as you feel you are
doing good.

                         TERESA

        Thank you, Father Ruiz.

                                            FADEOUT.

INT. TERESA'S ROOM AT THE CONVENT. TWO DAYS LATER.
EVENING.

Teresa   enters   after   completing   the   journey   from
Madrid, leaves her sandals at the door.

She sits at her desk, opens her journal. She reads
aloud as she writes.

                         TERESA

        "Today I returned from Madrid, the
long dusty journey. What glorious sights!

Sun, sky, forest, village streets, bustling yet peaceful.

EXT. VILLAGE STREET WITH TAVERN. EVENING.

                    TERESA (V.O.)

"I took the long way home, riding quietly around the village, listening to the sounds of families at dinner, the merchants closing shop for the night. The tavern was full of laughter and music, a few clanking pots but no loud arguments.

INT. TERESA' ROOM AT THE CONVENT. CONTINUOUS.

Teresa stops writing for a moment, sipping water.

                    TERESA (V.O.)

"I have not forgotten the purpose of my trip, to visit with the Inquisitor, the rector of the Cathedral in Madrid.

                    (MORE)

                 TERESA (V.O.) (CONT'D)

He seems genuinely interested in our village, although I think he tries to hide his interest in order to seem objective.

"Who would tell him we are teaching 'sex education' here? Perhaps he is right -- I should try not to be curious about the source of the rumor. All the same, I felt worried until he heard Elsa's letter.

"When I left the interview, he seemed satisfied that we are doing our best to do God's work here. I rode home with a light heart, full of ideas for ways to celebrate God's wonderful plan for us as well as our duties as Christians."

FADEOUT TO DARKNESS.

EXT. YARD OUTSIDE CONVENT IN AVILA. AFTERNOON.

In the background Teresa and the sisters are preparing the area for the group meeting, as villagers enter and seat themselves.

In the foreground Senor Mariposa is chasing a village girl who does not like him.

MARIPOSA

Senorita!

ROSA

Good day, senor Mariposa.

MARIPOSA

You look especially lovely.

ROSA

Thank you.

MARIPOSA

How are your parents?

She does not answer. He lunges forward and takes her arm roughly, insistently.

Answer me! Talk to me!

ROSA

Let go of me, senor!

She pulls away and walks quickly toward her parents.

ROSA (CONT'D)

Stay away from me, senor Mariposa! Mama,
tell him to stay away from me!

MARIPOSA

I want to marry your daughter! You should
be grateful to me!

MAMA

(diplomatically)

We are honored, senor Mariposa, by your
offer. But ROSA does not seem ready to
make such a decision, even for her own
good.

ROSA

Please! Help me! Tell him to go away.

PAPA

She does not want to marry you,
Senor. I do not wish to force her into a
marriage that frightens her.

MARIPOSA

She should not be frightened! I am
a respected citizen! I own the water
mill!

A moment as the parents look at the daughter, who is
clearly repelled by Mariposa.

PAPA

I think ROSA has decided, senor.
Please do not bother her anymore.

Teresa and Beatrice have noticed the interaction between Senor Mariposa and the girl.

                    TERESA

          (to Sister Beatrice) Let us find
     chairs for these people.

Beatrice seats Senor Mariposa on one side of the meeting area, and the girl with her parents on the other side.

                    BEATRICE

     We are ready, Sister Teresa!

The villagers rumble around, finding their places. A lone woman, LADY Gonzales, is leaning against the wall.

                    TERESA

          This lady should have a chair.
     Which one of you good men will give her
     a place to sit?

The men look at each other. Lope, seated alone in the back, watches the interaction with curiosity, embarrassed by his own reluctance and the behavior of the other men.

                    LADY

     I shall stand, Sister.

Teresa nods. A moment of disappointment and bewilderment passes over Teresa's face.

                    TERESA

          Last time we spoke about peace-
     making. We are pleased the week has been
     peaceful. The constable did not bring us
     any persons to chastise.

ELSA

We heard you were summoned to Madrid.

TERESA

Yes.

Murmurs, a rumble of displeasure ripples through the
group.

ELSA

Why did they summon you, Sister?

TERESA

The Madrid church official is
concerned about our weekly meetings.

A hush falls over the group.

The Inquisitor was displeased
because he heard we are teaching "sex
education."

LADY GONZALEZ

Somebody has to teach it!

All turn to look at her.

Unless you prefer your husbands go to the
whores!

Some of the men smile in spite of themselves.
Hurrumphs from wives and widows, giving the men stern
looks.

ELSA

How dare you suggest such a thing,
here at God's house!

                    MARITZA

          Shameful!

The group murmurs, a deeper rumble.

                    TERESA

          Can we not discuss this problem
          together? Surely we are not the only
          village with taverns and prostitutes.

                    BEATRICE

          Perhaps we could think on Mary
          Magdalena and the way Jesus loved her.

                    TERESA

          (nodding in agreement)

          Yes. We have the Lord's instruction
          in the scripture - "Let he who is without
          sin cast the first stone."

Carlos tosses a pebble along the ground. Everyone
else turns to look but Carlos behaves as if he too
is wondering who threw the pebble. Teresa smiles
indulgently.

                    TERESA (CONT'D)

          A sense of humor is a good thing.
          We all like to believe we are sinless.

                    LADY GONZALEZ

          The truth is we have all sinned, in
          our hearts if not in our deeds.

                    TERESA

          You bring wisdom with you. You have
          reflected on marriage?

LADY GONZALEZ

I know what it is to be happily married.

TERESA

We are pleased you have found happiness.

LADY GONZALEZ

I also know the pain of living
without love, with a man who seems like
a stranger. My husband went away to fight
in a Crusade. When he returned, he was a
changed man. Some days I feel as if a
stranger has taken his place.

MARITZA

My husband fought in the Crusade.

TERESA

Has he returned?

MARITZA

Yes, and he's much better!

Her friends giggle with her. Teresa is thoughtful.

TERESA

I did not know about the problem of
men returning from war. Have other men
changed a great deal?

LOPE

War changes people, Sister.

TERESA

Tell us about how your experience.

LOPE

I had to kill more than once. Many
nights I have bad dreams. The dreams

continue, but I try to turn my attention
to living.One should concentrate on the
living not the dead.

He looks at his wife. She touches his arm.

                    LOPE (CONT'D)

     I have told my wife about my
experiences. I wish I could feel
contentment again. Every time I begin to
feel happy with my family, my heart stops
me. "Who am I to be happy?" This is the
question I ask.

                    TERESA

You ask me?

                    LOPE

     Yes. Is it right to be happy when so many
have died?

                    TERESA

     God means us to have great joy. Why
would He have given us the ability to
love, if He did not wish for us to be
joyful?

                    MARITZA

     Hedonism is condemned by the Holy Church,
Sister.

                    TERESA

     Hedonism is different from joy in
living, joy in the gifts of God. The
greater sin may be pessimism, denial of
joy.

                    TERESA (CONT'D)

     How many people have been affected by the
war?

The crowd responds, mostly in the affirmative.

                    TERESA (CONT'D)

          We could have another meeting that
     discusses the effects of the war and how
     to deal with the effect on the families
     in our village. Would you like to have
     such a meeting?

Several women indicate assent.

                    TERESA (CONT'D)

          Good! Let us close our meeting with
     a moment of silent thanks to God.

After the meeting, people linger to talk in small
clusters. SENOR MARIPOSA stares at ROSA, hovering
behind her parents.

MARIPOSA approaches Teresa as she starts to leave the
meeting. A young novice, SISTER LUISA, observes their
conversation discreetly.

                    MARIPOSA

          Sister, I have an urgent matter to
     discuss.

                    TERESA

     Yes?

                    MARIPOSA

     I want to marry that girl over there.

                    TERESA

          Marriage is an honorable estate.
     You are . . . ?

                    MARIPOSA

     I am Senor Mariposa. I own the water
mill at the east end of our village.

                     TERESA

     The water mill?

                    MARIPOSA

     We supply water to the entire village.

                     TERESA

     Your   mill   is   important   to   the
welfare of our community. How may I help
you?

                    MARIPOSA

     Her parents gave their consent but
the girl refuses to obey.

                     TERESA

     The girl says no?

                    MARIPOSA

     She refuses to obey her parents.

                     TERESA

     Why would you want to marry a girl
who will not obey her parents and follow
custom?

                    MARIPOSA

     Look at her! She is beautiful!

                     TERESA

     We have other pretty girls in the
village.

                    MARIPOSA

     But she is the most beautiful! I
want my children to look like her.

                    TERESA

     I can understand your unhappiness
about the failed marriage proposal.

                   MARIPOSA

     The girl refuses to obey her parents!

                    TERESA

     She must feel strongly that she
does not want to marry you. Why would you
pursue such a woman?

                   MARIPOSA

                   (riled)

     I told you! I want my children to
be beautiful!

                    TERESA

     Beauty is a gift from God, like good
health. Are you healthy, sir?

                   MARIPOSA

                  (proudly)

     I have never been sick a day in my
life!

                    TERESA

     Then you are blessed by God! Why
are you so angry?

                   MARIPOSA

     (angrily) I am not angry!

                    TERESA

     I feel your anger penetrating my
body as we speak.

MARIPOSA

(backing away)

I did not expect such criticism
from a sister.

TERESA

I do not mean to be critical, sir.

MARIPOSA

Then why are you telling me this?

TERESA

Perhaps it is the only way I can
help you with your dilemma. Would you
like to hear my advice, or shall I keep
silent?

MARIPOSA

(reluctantly) What is your advice?

TERESA

Perhaps if you ask God to release
you from your anger, then you will be a
more attractive suitor.

MARIPOSA

You think she will accept my
proposal?

TERESA

I think not. But perhaps you will
find another woman, a woman who will
accept you as you are - when you have
found release from anger.

Mariposa walks away in silence. Teresa notices the
novice, Sister Luisa, who is still watching Senor
Mariposa.

INT. TERESA'S ROOM AT THE CONVENT. EVENING.

Teresa is writing in her journal. Sister Luisa knocks
at the door, carrying Teresa's evening meal.

                    TERESA

          Come in.

Sister LUISA enters and sets the meal on the desk
quietly.

                    LUISA

          Sister Teresa, here is a letter for you.

Teresa reaches for the envelope, notes the
handwriting.

                    TERESA

          From Toledo. When did it arrive?

                    LUISA

          In the afternoon. I did not find
time to bring you the letter until now.

                    TERESA

          Thank you, sister. You seem tired.
Is something wrong?

                    LUISA

          The cook is unhappy because we did
not receive a shipment of fish.

          Tonight we can offer only bread and
cheese.

                         TERESA

     This is more than adequate. Tell
the cook her bread is the best I have
ever tasted!

                         LUISA

Thank you, Sister Teresa!

Sister LUISA leaves, looking more cheerful. Teresa
opens the letter from her father.

                         TERESA

                  (reading aloud)

     "Your sister, Mira, and I enjoy
your letters. We are pleased that life at
the convent progresses smoothly, and that
you are well.

                     ALONSO (V.O.)

     "Now I am all alone here at the
villa. So quiet! Yesterday I told Mira:
the silence is deafening! I enjoy the
peace but miss the companionship of your
mother.

     "Our church has become host to a
noted painter and his assistant, a
journeyman painter.

INT. CHURCH SANCTUARY IN TOLEDO.

Domenikos is putting finishing touches on a painting
hanging in the sanctuary. Juan looks on.

                     ALONSO (V.O.)

     "We know the famous painter as
Domenikos the Greek, or simply El Greco.
The Greek is said to be temperamental but

his paintings are admired by the Vatican.
He is away now, visiting Rome.

                    ALONSO (V.O.)

     "I hope you can arrange to visit us
soon in Toledo.

EXT. ALONSO'S FARM NEAR TOLEDO.

Alonso sits on his porch, writing the letter. He stops
to watch farm workers harvest grain.

                    ALONSO (V.O.)

     "The harvest has just begun and the
weather will be perfect. I think you'll
find   that   Toledo   has   changed   in
interesting   ways,   while   remaining   the
same comforting place it has always been
for us.

Alonso writes the letter.

                    ALONSO (V.O.)

     "I wish to settle the matter of our
property   in   Toledo.   As   you   know,   your
brothers and sisters have settled in town
with their families. Mira and her husband
have at last found a house they like for
a reasonable sum.

     "I would like you to have the villa.

INT. TERESA'S ROOM AT THE CONVENT. CONTINUOUS.

Teresa reacts with surprise, puts down the letter for
a moment, takes some water. Then she resumes reading
the letter .

                    ALONSO (V.O.)

     "You are my only unmarried daughter.

                    ALONSO (V.O.) (CONT'D)

    I would like to talk with you in
person and settle the property with a
legal document.

    "I have spoken with our local
priest. He assured me that other
monastics own property and they are not
necessarily required to give the property
to the Church.

    "We cannot predict what life will
bring, Teresa.

    "Your loving father, Alonso."

Teresa puts her head on her desk and sleeps.

EXT. ALONSO'S FARM. MORNING.

DREAM MONTAGE: sweeping panoramic views of her
father's villa, the fields, vineyards, stable.

From a distance Teresa sees her parents kneeling
before a simple altar, her father holding a wooden
crucifix.

Teresa runs to her father and they embrace warmly.
She gazes at his handsome face, holds his hands in
hers. In the dream he presses a small wooden cross
into her palm.

                    TERESA

    Father, has God spoken to you?

INT. TERESA'S ROOM AT THE CONVENT. CONTINUOUS.

Teresa awakens and looks at her hands, half expecting to find the small cross from her dream. Her hands are empty, her heart is full.

> SUPERIMPOSITION
> TO NEXT SCENE.

INT. CONFESSIONAL BOOTH IN CHURCH SANCTUARY, TOLEDO. TWO WEEKS LATER. MORNING.

> FATHER FRANCISCO

What would you like to discuss, Juan?

> JUAN

You know I live here in Toledo, and I am a painter?

> FATHER FRANCISCO

Yes, I know.

> JUAN

In Valencia I worked for years as a journeyman painter, respected by my colleagues. When I first moved here my new master the Greek made me feel like a beginner again!

At first the Greek made me spend all my time building frames for his canvases, then a scaffold to permit him to paint a fresco above your confessional, Father Francisco.

> FADEOUT TO
> WHITE.

INT. FLASHBACK: ARTISTS' WORKROOM INSIDE CHURCH.
MORNING.

                    DOMENIKOS

      Juan! You must build a scaffold for me.

                    JUAN

      Why?

                    DOMENIKOS

      For a fresco.

                    JUAN

      You need a scaffold to paint a
fresco?

Domenikos' brows knit together, showing he is annoyed
by the comment. Juan does not tell him he is hungry
because he did not eat breakfast.

                    JUAN (CONT'D)

      Pardon me, Master, but I do not
understand.

                    DOMENIKOS

      Father Francisco wants a new fresco
above his confessional. I am not going to
paint a great painting while teetering on
a ladder.

He looks at Juan searchingly.

                    DOMENIKOS (CONT'D)

      Do you know how to build a scaffold?

                    JUAN

      Yes, of course. My father is a
carpenter. I helped my father build one
when I was ten years old.

                    DOMENIKOS

          Good. Start work on it today.

Domenikos sets to work gathering brushes for a
commission, Jesus in a purple-red robe in the midst
of a group. He mutters something.

                      JUAN

          May I ask you a question, Master

                    DOMENIKOS

          Ask.

                      JUAN

          How did you know you would be a
great and famous painter?

                    DOMENIKOS

          I used to believe that God decides.
Now I know that a famous person may be
lonely yet keep the loneliness a secret,
except perhaps from their confessor.

Domenikos mutters again.

                      JUAN

          What did you say, Master?

                    DOMENIKOS

          The Vatican has painters hanging
from scaffolds. If they can do it, so can
we! Tomorrow I shall go to Rome and see
how they do it.

Exit Domenikos. END OF FLASHBACK.

                              FADE TO WHITE.

INT. CONFESSIONAL IN CHURCH SANCTUARY. CONTINUOUS.

Juan's confessional conversation with Father
Francisco continues.

                              JUAN

          It seems a long time since
     Domenikos went away. I miss him, miss his
     constant presence. After a time I forgot
     about his criticisms, his silence when
     displeased.   I   miss   his   occasional
     kindnesses, and his love for painting.

          While Domenikos is away, I work
     every day in the church - building the
     scaffold, painting highlights and
     shadows in the drapery in his paintings.
     Alone I painted the soldier's helmet in
     the new commission portraying Jesus in a
     red-purple robe.

                                SUPERIMPOSITION TO
                                    NEXT SCENE.

INT. CHURCH IN TOLEDO. SAME DAY, AFTERNOON.

Teresa enters the church. She is dressed in street
clothing, so her status as a monastic is not apparent
from her dress.

The door is open, the sanctuary empty. As Teresa walks
into the entrance hall she sees a painting above an
altar. She stops to look and pray. She is not aware
that Juan has seen her and entered the sanctuary
quietly.

                              JUAN

          Good day, Senora.

Teresa opens her eyes, mildly startled. She looks at
Juan.

                         JUAN (CONT'D)

          I did not wish to startle you.
     Forgive me. When you walked into the
     sanctuary, I saw you.

TERESA

I've had quite a journey today.

JUAN

Where did you start your travels?

TERESA

In Avila.

JUAN

What do you think of our new
painting?

TERESA

Beautiful! It lifts my spirit!

He nods, briefly, looks at the painting as if for the
first time.

TERESA (CONT'D)

Do you know the name of the painter?

JUAN

Yes. He lives here in Toledo.

TERESA

Is he a parishioner?

JUAN

Yes, you might say that. He works
here in the church.

TERESA

I see. Where do you come from?

JUAN

I came here from Valencia. And you?

                    TERESA

     My family lives in Toledo. I am
visiting them for a few weeks, then I go
home.

                    JUAN

     Home?

                    TERESA

     To Avila. I am a sister at the
convent.

                    JUAN

     You, a nun?

He laughs, then stops himself.

                    JUAN (CONT'D)

     Forgive me! You are too attractive
to be a nun!

                    TERESA

     But I am! I am a teacher at the
convent.

                    JUAN

     Have you ever been married?

                    TERESA

     Only to our Lord, Jesus Christ. Why
do you smile?

                    JUAN

     I am surprised that an attractive
woman like you did not marry --- a
wealthy nobleman!

                    TERESA

     (charmed in spite of herself)
     Thank you, sir.

                    JUAN

          Am I permitted to talk with you?

                    TERESA

          I am allowed to talk with any
person.

                    JUAN

          Good! Would you like to see more
paintings?

                    TERESA

          You mean the paintings here in the
chapel?

                    JUAN

          These, and others. I keep the
church's collection of art works.

                    TERESA

          Are you the painter?

                    JUAN

          Yes! I painted part of this
painting, and several others in the
church's collection. Now I am working on
a section of a new painting while my
master is away in Rome.

He takes her by the arm, then he stops himself.

          Forgive me, I am not accustomed to
talking with nuns. The priest here
behaves informally with me. What shall I
call you?

                    TERESA

          You may call me Teresa.

She takes his arm, surprised by how natural the
gesture feels to her.

                    JUAN

        My name is Juan.

INT. CHAPEL. CONTINUOUS.

They walk into the chapel. Teresa stops before a
painting in an alcove.

                    JUAN

        This large painting near the altar
    was painted by the Greek.

They stand before the painting in silence.

                    JUAN (CONT'D)

        What do you think?

                    TERESA

        (pulling herself as if from a trance)

        It's difficult to describe what I
    feel. Such beautiful flying and floating!
    Who is the knight?

                    JUAN

        He was a respected citizen of Toledo.

                    TERESA

        How did he die?

                    JUAN

        The Inquisition. The count died
    before I came to Toledo, so I could not
    meet him in person. I met his brother.
    They say the two men are very much alike.

                    TERESA

     Such a handsome face!

She inwardly chastises herself.

                    TERESA (CONT'D)

     Forgive me.

                    JUAN

     Why?

                    TERESA

     We try not to judge people by
appearances.

                    JUAN

     Surely you are allowed to
appreciate beautiful things and
beautiful faces!

                    TERESA

     But we must not be overshadowed by
beauty. We try to appreciate without
succumbing to . . .

                    JUAN

     To passion?

Teresa is silent momentarily.

                    TERESA

     Love is not only passion. Much of
love involves will, the decision to do
the will of God.

                    JUAN

     And for those of us who do not seek
to be holy? Can we not include passion in
our lives?

                    TERESA

     I think passion is part of the
decision to marry -- for most people. But
when passion wanes, then the trouble
starts.

                    JUAN

     You counsel married couples?

                    TERESA

     Yes. We hold special meetings for
couples and families from the village.

                    JUAN

     Do many attend your special meetings?

                    TERESA

     Dozens! There are too many . . . We
do not have enough staff to counsel
people individually.

                    JUAN

     Did you start to say the village
has too many couples with problems?

                    TERESA

          (reluctantly)

     Yes.

                    JUAN

     No wonder you are not keen on marriage.

                    TERESA

     I am past the age when girls must marry.

                    JUAN

     You seem healthy.

                    TERESA

     Yes,   thank   God.   Instead   of   a
spinster, I became a teacher.

He is tempted to steal a kiss but he does not. Instead
he gazes at her face, touches her hand resting on his
arm.

                    JUAN

     Perhaps you gave up too easily.

                    TERESA

     I did not give up anything. I was
drawn into a greater Love.

He touches her hands as if to memorize them.

                    JUAN

     Does your family approve of your
vocation?

                    TERESA

     Who would protect them from the
Inquisition if I were not a nun?

                    JUAN

     What brought you here to Toledo?

                    TERESA

     A letter from my father. He is alone
now since my mother died. He sounded
lonely. I have not seen him in a long
time.

                    JUAN

     I hope I'll see you again during
your visit.

                    TERESA

     I'd enjoy it!

                    JUAN

          How long will you stay?

                   TERESA

          Two, maybe three weeks. I'm on
     leave from the convent.

                    JUAN

          Come to the Sunday service.

                   TERESA

          I can come if my father comes to
     worship. He is expecting me soon!

Juan kisses her hand.

                    JUAN

          Until Sunday!

                                   FADE OUT.

INTERIOR. SAME CHAPEL. SUNDAY, TWO DAYS LATER.

Music plays as the service concludes and people start
to leave the chapel. TERESA, ALONSO and Teresa's
sister MIRA join the line of people exiting.

From the other side of the chapel, JUAN the painter
watches TERESA and her family as they stop to converse
with the parish priest, FATHER FRANCISCO.

As JUAN walks near the small gathering, he overhears
TERESA speak to the priest.

                   TERESA

          I have work to do, the work of God.

MIRA nods approvingly.

                              MIRA

     When she was a novice, TERESA
searched her heart and decided she
belonged to the Lord. We cannot quarrel
with her decision.

ALONSO seems less sanguine. He notices Juan first,
before Mira sees him.

                            TERESA

     Father, Mira, this is Juan. He is
the artist here at the church.

                       FATHER FRANCISCO

     Juan works diligently. He is the
favorite assistant of the Greek, the
famous artist who has been noticed by the
Vatican.

                            MIRA

     Is he here?

                       FATHER FRANCISCO

     The Greek? He has gone back to
Italy, at the Pope's request.

MIRA is impressed.

                            MIRA

     The Pope has heard of our little
parish?

                       FATHER FRANCISCO

     Because of the Greek artist and his
masterful paintings.

                            JUAN

     Perhaps he will visit us again - someday.

MIRA continues chatting with the priest.

                    ALONSO

          (his   tone   friendlier   than   his
     words):
          TERESA   told   us   about   you,   young
     man.

                    JUAN

     You have a remarkable daughter, senor.

TERESA smiles warmly at JUAN and takes his arm without
thinking. JUAN quickly places his hand on hers, to
prevent her taking her hand away.

                    JUAN (CONT'D)

     I   would   like   to   get   to   know   her   much
     better.

                    ALONSO

     (speaking softly so Mira will not hear)

     Will you come to dinner tonight?

TERESA nearly jumps with surprise but JUAN holds her
hand firmly.

                    JUAN

     Yes!

                    ALONSO

          Come at seven. Our villa is on the
     edge of town, on the road to Madrid.

JUAN nods his assent.

Alonso swiftly retrieves Mira and guides her toward
the door before another word can be spoken. Teresa
lingers a moment, then follows. She looks back at
Juan, who waves, then Teresa exits with Alonso and
Mira.

INT. SANCHEZ FAMILY HOME, DINING ROOM. SAME DAY, EVENING.

Mira and her husband are already seated together at the table. Alonso sits to the side.

SOUND CUE: Ideally Alonso plays his guitar or other musical instrument. Otherwise, Spanish guitar music may be played to cover the scene transition and set the mood.

Teresa, who has been setting the table, speaks to her family.

TERESA

Juan will be here soon. We should not start dinner without him.

Teresa sees Juan at the door and goes to welcome him. At a nod from Alonso, Teresa guides Juan to his seat. They sit next to each other. Juan kisses her hand.

MIRA

Welcome to our home, Juan.

TERESA

She is Mira, one of my sisters. She keeps my father from getting lonely here at the farm.

JUAN

Thank you for your welcome. I am happy to be invited to your family home.

Alonso sits at the table, and closes his eyes for a moment. Everybody else puts their hands together for the evening prayer.

ALONSO

Lord, I ask you to bless my family, our guest, Juan the artist, and this dinner. We are grateful that Teresa arrived safely.

Mira takes a bit of food, and everybody else follows.

MONTAGE: Images from the dinner table gathering, views through the window of changing light. Then a glimpse of after- dinner activity: Alonso playing guitar, Mira and her husband playing cards.

Guitar music continues to play, creating a link between scenes in the montage.

SUPERIMPOSITION
TO EXTERIOR.

EXT. GARDEN OUTSIDE THE SANCHEZ FAMILY HOME. LATER SAME EVENING.

Juan and Teresa stroll together outside in the twilight. Lanterns may provide additional light.

TERESA

Tell me about yourself, Juan.

JUAN

What else do you want to know?

TERESA

I want to know you! Tell me how you came to be a painter. Many men would like to have your position, isn't that true?

JUAN

Yes, it's a very good position for a painter, usually. Sometimes I spend all day building a scaffold so my master can

paint on the ceiling! But that work has
to be done.

                    TERESA

You are also a carpenter?

                    JUAN

My father is a carpenter. I learned
the trade from him. Then he got me an
apprenticeship with a respected church
painter in Valencia, my home town.

                    TERESA

How did you come to Toledo?

                    JUAN

First I was promoted from
apprentice to journeyman painter, a big
step. I was accepted into the guild and
got my first solo assignment, to paint a
portrait of Jesus.

                    TERESA

How wonderful!

                    JUAN

Yes, that project meant a great
deal to me. For years I worked as a
journeyman painter, not earning much
money but respected by the community.

Then the opportunity came to work
here with a well-known icon painter. My
master recommended me for the
opportunity. When I asked him why, he
said I was becoming as skilled a painter
as he was. So it was time for me to have
a new challenge.

(MORE)

JUAN (CONT'D)

And that's how I came to be assistant to "the Greek," Domenikos.

Now you tell me something about yourself.

TERESA

You already know most of my story. You've met my family.

JUAN

Tell me about your work at the convent.

TERESA

Every week we have meetings with the villagers. If the constable has brought people to be chastised, one of the sisters talks with them individually. It is like confession but less formal. With the others who are not in trouble we have an open discussion.

After the community meeting, I go to evening prayer and the evening meal. Often I write or talk with the sisters in the evening.

JUAN

It sounds like a full day. You would miss life as a teacher and counselor if you were to leave.

TERESA

What are you saying?

JUAN

Have you ever thought about what married life would be like?

TERESA

I have counselled many couples.

JUAN

Have there been any happy marriages in your experience?

TERESA

Sometimes a villager speaks of happiness in married life.

JUAN

I don't want to frighten you, Teresa. But you must know I am falling in love with you.

He takes her hands and kisses them tenderly.

There's no need to hurry. You'll be here in Toledo for a few weeks.

TERESA

Yes, I will.

JUAN

If you want me to stop talking about this, tell me now.

TERESA

I don't want you to stop! Suddenly I do not understand myself.

JUAN

Do you miss your life at the convent?

TERESA

No! I confess I haven't thought about them since you accepted father's invitation to dinner. I wonder at myself, at my change of heart.

                    JUAN

     I'm very glad to hear you say so.
I'll tell you a secret. I have a ring my
mother gave me.

                  TERESA

     She is alive?

                    JUAN

     Yes, she's still alive. It's a ring
she received from my father before they
were betrothed, a friendship ring. Would
you like to see it?

                  TERESA

     Yes!

Juan draws the ring from a pocket.

          It's lovely. What is the stone?

                    JUAN

     An emerald. Do you like it?

                  TERESA

     Yes, Juan, I like it.

                    JUAN

     Then you may try it.

She puts the ring on her finger.

                  TERESA

     It fits!

                    JUAN

     I thought it might fit. I cannot
wear it, it doesn't fit my fingers.

                  TERESA

     A friendship ring?

                    JUAN

          Yes. It's yours, if you'll wear it.

                    TERESA

          Thank you, Juan. It's beautiful!

                    JUAN

                    (encouraged)

          I want to be with you more than
     anything, but I don't want to press you.

He offers his arm, and she takes it. They walk toward
the sunset, to Juan's horse and carriage.

                    TERESA

          Will   you   come   to   dinner   again
     tomorrow?

                    JUAN

          Yes, of course. But tomorrow is my
     day off. Would you like to ride around
     Toledo with me in my carriage? I can come
     about ten o'clock tomorrow, if that's
     convenient.

                    TERESA

          Yes! I'll be ready.

                              SUPERIMPOSITION
                              TO NEXT SCENE.

EXT. OUTSIDE THE SANCHEZ FAMILY ESTATE. NEXT DAY, MORNING.

The next day Juan drives up in his carriage. Teresa comes out to meet him. He helps her into the carriage and they drive off into the morning sunshine.

MONTAGE: Images of Toledo - a minaret on the road into town, the bazaar, the town market.

Lively peasant music - recorders, flutes - interspersed with dance music on guitar plays over the montage.

EXT. TOWN MARKET. LATER SAME MORNING.

Juan and Teresa walk through the market, buying food and placing it in a large basket carried by Juan. Teresa holds Juan's arm.

                    FRUIT MERCHANT

        Good day, Juan! Who is your lady
    friend?

                    JUAN

        This is Teresa. She is a very
    special friend.

                    FRUIT MERCHANT

        First time I've seen you with a
    "lady friend!" Life is good? Yes?

Teresa smiles, enjoying the teasing.

                    JUAN

        Yes, life is good!

                    TERESA

        We'd like to buy an assortment of
    your fruit, for my father and his family.

FRUIT MERCHANT

Who is your father?

TERESA

Alonso Sanchez. His villa is on the edge of town.

FRUIT MERCHANT

Yes, I know the villa. Let me see, an assortment of our best fruit for Juan and his lady friend.

He chooses fruit from his stand and places it in a basket.

EXT. TOWN MARKET. LATER SAME MORNING.

A small group of musicians is playing at an open space in the market. Townspeople dance to the music.

Juan and Teresa stop at a bench to watch. They sit and Juan places the basket of fruit to the side. He puts his arm around Teresa as they listen to the music. She leans against him, tentatively at first, then with more comfort and assurance.

JUAN

Do you like our folk music?

TERESA

Yes, very much. It's been a long time since I listened to music like this.

JUAN

I like watching the dancers too.

                    TERESA

     I like to watch. Nuns are not
permitted to join in the dancing.

                    JUAN

We will watch.

                              SUPERIMPOSITION
                               TO NEXT SCENE.

INT. SANCHEZ FAMILY HOME. SAME DAY, LATE AFTERNOON.

Teresa and Juan arrive with the basket filled with
food from the town market. Mira greets them.

                    JUAN

     Have we arrived on time? You
haven't started dinner yet, have you?

                    MIRA

Not yet.

                    TERESA

     We brought food, Mira. Can you use
this?

Juan presents the basket of food.

                    JUAN

     Here is our offering for dinner.

Mira sorts through the basket.

                    MIRA

     Fruits, vegetables, yes. What's
this? Fresh fish! Fresh-baked cakes! We
will have a fine dinner tonight! Thank
you.

Mira notices the ring on Teresa's finger. She reaches
for Teresa's hand.

                    MIRA (CONT'D)

        What's this, Teresa? A ring?!!

                    TERESA

        Yes, it's a friendship ring from
Juan.

                    MIRA

        It's beautiful. You are generous,
Juan.

                    JUAN

        It belonged to my mother. My father
gave it to her as a friendship ring
before they were engaged.

Mira is silent for a moment.

                    MIRA

        That's a nice story. Excuse me, I
must get dinner ready. The cook is
waiting for me.

Mira exits.

                    JUAN

        She doesn't like the ring.

                    TERESA

        She likes the ring. Mira is afraid
of the Inquisition. She looks to me as
the family's protector.

                    JUAN

        Why? Is she at risk?

                    TERESA

     My father's father was a Jew. Now
that mother is gone, Mira is afraid that
we may come under scrutiny. Some of my
other siblings feel the same way. To have
a nun in the family is reassuring to
them. They believe the Inquisition has
left us alone because I am a nun.

                              SUPERIMPOSITION
                              TO NEXT SCENE.

EXT. GARDEN OUTSIDE SANCHEZ FAMILY HOME. SAME DAY,
EVENING.

Teresa and Juan walk in the garden.

                    JUAN

     It was a delicious dinner! Your
sister and the cook make a very good
team.

                    TERESA

     We inspired them with our purchases
from the Town Market.

                    JUAN

     It was a good day, wasn't it?

                    TERESA

     It was a wonderful day, Juan! I
enjoyed your company. Do you have to go
back to work tomorrow?

                    JUAN

     I can take some time off. Tomorrow
I will stop into the church to tell the

priest I'm taking some time to show you
around Toledo. In the afternoon, I can
pick you up in my carriage.

                    TERESA

     That would be delightful! But are
you sure you can take time off, Juan?
Your work is important.

                    JUAN

     My master is in Italy, as you know.
I can put in more time after you return
to your convent. Unless you have changed
your mind and plan to stay here . . . ?

                    TERESA

     I'm expected back at the convent in
a few weeks. I must return.

                    JUAN

     I understand. But you should know
that I would like to marry you.

                    TERESA

Marry me?!!

                    JUAN

     Love is a very good reason to marry.
I want to marry you more than anything,
but I don't want to press you.

                    TERESA

You speak of love?

                    JUAN

     I've told you I'm in love with you.
Forgive me, but I sense you feel the same
way.

TERESA

I'm surprised at myself. I did not
believe I could feel this way about
anyone but our Lord Jesus.

JUAN

(encouraged)

So you do feel love for me?

TERESA

I feel deep love for you, Juan. But
I have never before considered marriage
to a man. We take vows like vows of
marriage to the Church when we become
nuns.

JUAN

You take your vows seriously, I know.

TERESA

I cannot marry honorably without
first getting permission from my family,
from the convent sisters and, above all,
from the Inquisitor.

JUAN

Please, get permission!

SUPERIMPOSITION
TO NEXT SCENE.

INT. SANCHEZ FAMILY HOME. TWO WEEKS LATER, AFTERNOON.

Alonso and Mira work on organizing the farm's finances. Enter Teresa.

> ALONSO

Teresa, you are home early. Is Juan at work?

> TERESA

Yes, he has some work he must do today. And I want to talk with you privately.

> ALONSO

What is it, my dear?

> TERESA

Father, Juan has asked me to be his fiancée.

> ALONSO

Wonderful! This is wonderful news, my dear!

> MIRA

You've known each other only two weeks!

> TERESA

I know, but I feel as if I've known Juan a long time. He feels it too.

> MIRA

But Teresa, you are married to the Church! You said yourself, you have work to do!

> ALONSO

You have my blessing, Teresa. I am happy for you and Juan!

Alonso embraces daughter Teresa.

                    MIRA

     Teresa, what will you tell the
sisters? What will you say to the
Inquisitor in Madrid?

                    TERESA

     I will write to him and explain that
I have been called in a different
direction.

                    MIRA

     What will happen to us? We are safe
from the Inquisition because of your
position in the church.

                    TERESA

     You are loyal Christians. You go to
church and to confession.

                    MIRA

     How can you be so selfish?

                    TERESA

     Is it selfish to go where love
leads?

                    MIRA

     I think it is.

                    TERESA

     I'm not sure. It may be God's way
of sending me in a different direction.

                    ALONSO

     Mira, don't you think your sister
deserves some earthly happiness in this
life?

Mira is silent.

ALONSO (CONT'D)

My dear, you have a husband whom
you love. Yes?

Mira nods. This much is true.

ALONSO (CONT'D)

You have a comfortable house. Yes?

MIRA

Yes, father. This is my fear
speaking. Aren't you afraid, Father?

ALONSO

We have enjoyed Teresa's protection
for many years. We have a good
relationship with the parish priest. We
go to church and confession regularly.
What more can be asked of us?

MIRA

So you believe the troubles with
Grandfather's Judaism are in the past?

ALONSO

Yes. We are not practicing Jews. We
are practicing Christians.

Mira embraces Teresa.

MIRA

I will try to be happy for you,
Teresa. I hope you will always be as
happy as you are today.

TERESA

Thank you, Mira.

                    ALONSO

     Now I have an announcement of my
own. I would like to give the villa to
Teresa and Juan.

                    MIRA

     The villa!

                    TERESA

     I can stay at Juan's house, after I
make my departure from the convent.

                    ALONSO

     I think my solution is better,
Teresa.

                    MIRA

     Where will you stay, Father?

                    TERESA

     Please stay with us, father, here
at the villa.

Alonso smiles gently.

                    ALONSO

     Perhaps I will. I can help you learn
to run the farm.

                    MIRA

     I can help too.

                    ALONSO

     We will see how it goes. If we are
uncomfortable all here together, I've an
invitation from one of your brothers to
live with him and his wife.

Alonso gives a wrapped document to Teresa.

                    ALONSO (CONT'D)

Here is the deed to the villa. The farm's documents are being drawn up. We will continue to run the farm until you wish to take over.

                    MIRA

I hope you will enjoy being a farmer, Teresa. It will be a big change for you.

                    TERESA

Yes, it will be a change. First I must get permission to marry from the convent and the Church.

                    ALONSO

Do you anticipate any problems?

                    TERESA

I don't know anyone who has done this. I don't know what to expect.

                    ALONSO

Father Francisco says the Church releases those who are called to marry.

                    TERESA

I hope they will release me honorably.

                    ALONSO

I hope so too!

He embraces Teresa.

SUPERIMPOSITION
TO NEXT SCENE.

EXT. GARDEN OUTSIDE SANCHEZ HOME. SAME DAY, LATE
AFTERNOON.

Teresa walks with Juan in the garden.

                        TERESA

     Juan, I told my father and Mira that
we want to marry. My father gave us his
blessing.

                        JUAN

     That's very good!

He kisses her.

                        TERESA

     Even   Mira   has   accepted   our
decision. And my father has given me the
villa. So we can live there!

                        JUAN

     The villa is much bigger than my
small house. Your father is generous!
Will he stay here too?

                        TERESA

     Yes, I told him he would stay with
us.

                        JUAN

     They say three is too many for a
first house.

                        TERESA

     He needs a place to live! He can
help me run the farm.

                    JUAN

     I see. We will have to consider
this, but first you need permission to
leave the convent.

                    TERESA

     Yes. Getting permission from the
sisters could be tricky.

                    JUAN

     Why?

                    TERESA

     Recently   we've   been   holding
meetings with the villagers.

                    JUAN

     You told me.

                    TERESA

     I'm the leader for the meetings.
Without me, the meetings may fall apart.

                    JUAN

     Isn't there someone else who could lead
the meetings?

Teresa reflects for a moment.

                    TERESA

     Yes, I know a sister who could take
my place.

                    JUAN

     Will you miss leading the meetings?

                    TERESA

     Not nearly as much as I'll miss you!

Juan embraces her.

                    JUAN

     I will miss you too! These few weeks
together have changed my life. I'm so
happy, and so sad to see you go. Will you
write to me?

                   TERESA

     Yes! But first I must write to the
Inquisitor for permission to marry.

                                SUPERIMPOSITION
                                 TO NEXT SCENE.

INT. CONVENT ENTRANCE. A FEW DAYS LATER, AFTERNOON.

Teresa arrives, carrying a bag. Beatrice greets her
at the open door.

                   TERESA

     Sister Beatrice, I want you to be
the first to know my news.

                  BEATRICE

     I have news for you as well, Teresa,
news you will be happy to hear.

                   TERESA

     Then you speak first.

                  BEATRICE

     No, you go first, Sister Teresa.
You have been gone almost a month. We
missed you!

Enter Sister Jana.

                    JANA

     You returned, Sister Teresa! I
thought you were gone forever!

                    BEATRICE

     What kind of greeting is that,
Jana?

                     TERESA

           (to Beatrice)

     Let's go to the yard. We can talk
there.

EXT. YARD OUTSIDE THE CONVENT. IMMEDIATELY AFTERWARD.

                     TERESA

     It's been a full time, these past
weeks in Toledo, a time full of love. I
have fallen in love with a man, a painter
at my family's parish church. He has
asked me to marry him, and I accepted
him.

                    BEATRICE

     I'm overwhelmed, Teresa! You could
push me over with one breath!

                     TERESA

     Please don't be angry, Beatrice.

                    BEATRICE

     I'm not angry, only very surprised!
This is a big change in your life, in all
of our lives here at the convent.

                     TERESA

     Yes, it will affect the convent. I
hope you will take over the weekly
meetings with the villagers when I have
left.

BEATRICE

Where will you live? What is this miracle man's name?

TERESA

His name is Juan. He lives and works in Toledo, so we will stay there. My father has given us the family villa, and he will stay there too.

BEATRICE

Is it big enough for three?

TERESA

The villa is big enough for several people.

BEATRICE

This is wonderful! Surely the Church will permit you to leave honorably, now that you are called to the life of a married woman!

TERESA

I hope so. I'll write to the Inquisitor at the Cathedral in Madrid, telling him the whole story. And I will recommend you as my successor in teaching the community and the nuns.

BEATRICE

It's an honor, Teresa. I will not forget this.

TERESA

Now, tell me your happy news.

BEATRICE

News of a betrothal in the village.
Sister Luisa has taken a liking to Senor
Mariposa. You remember him?

TERESA

The man from the water mill? He was
so angry when the village girl refused
him!

BEATRICE

Yes, that is Senor Mariposa. He has
proposed to Sister Luisa and she has
accepted him, if she can get permission
to leave the convent honorably.

TERESA

That is good news! She will need
permission from the Church. Perhaps I can
plead her case.

BEATRICE

Perfect! With your help, she will
succeed!

TERESA

Senor Mariposa will be a happier
man, I hope.

BEATRICE

That is my hope too! Would you like
to speak with Sister Luisa?

TERESA

Yes, let me speak with her.

Beatrice goes to the door, where Luisa is waiting.
Enter SISTER LUISA.

TERESA

Sister, I understand you wish to leave the convent in order to marry.

LUISA

Yes, Sister Teresa. I wish to make myself a good wife for Pepe. He has been so kind to me!

TERESA

Tell me, how did you come to know and appreciate Pepe?

LUISA

At first I felt compassion for him. He seemed so alone. The townspeople turned against him, even though he owns the water mill. I tried talking to him. He didn't say much at first, not a word against the sisters or the townspeople.

Then he began to tell me about himself, about how hard he and his father worked to make the water mill successful. He even told me some funny stories about himself.

TERESA

So he has a sense of humor?

LUISA

Oh yes, Pepe can be funny! He charmed me with his stories and, one day, he asked me if I'd like to marry him. I said I needed time to think about it.

TERESA

How did he respond?

                         LUISA

     He was quiet. I think he was
disappointed. I did not see him for a
time, and I missed his companionship. The
next time I saw him he was kind. That's
when I decided I would like to be his
wife.

                        TERESA

     He sounds like a changed man! The
entire village would thank you if they
knew the story!

                         LUISA

     If he is changed, it is because he
decided to be different. I did not change
him, not much. I learned to appreciate
him and maybe that helped him change.

                        TERESA

     This is very good news, Sister
Luisa.

                        (MORE)

                   TERESA (CONT'D)

     I'll tell Father Ruiz in Madrid
about you and Pepe, with your permission.

                         LUISA

     Oh yes, I never dreamed you would
speak for us, Sister Teresa! Thank you so
much!

                        TERESA

     I too have been called to the life
of a married woman. We are both in need
of permission to leave the convent.

INT. TERESA'S ROOM AT THE CONVENT. NEXT DAY. MORNING.

Sister Beatrice listens as Teresa reads aloud from her letter to the Inquisitor.

                    TERESA

               (reading aloud)

          "Father Ruiz, I am writing to you because a wonderful thing has happened. A good, kind man has fallen in love with me and proposed marriage! He is a painter who works at the Cathedral Church in Toledo. Juan is a faithful Christian as well as a gifted painter. He works with the well- known painter, El Greco."

                    TERESA (CONT'D)

               (to Beatrice)

          Do you think it's too much information?

                    BEATRICE

          I think it's good to tell him about Juan.

                    TERESA

          "My widowed father has given me the villa where he lives. So Juan and I will have a large house. My father also plans to give me the farm he manages, so I will have a busy and purposeful life."

                    TERESA (CONT'D)

          "I am asking your permission to leave the convent in order to marry Juan and live with him as a householder.

"Sister Beatrice can take my place
here at the convent. She attends our
weekly meetings and is a very capable
leader. The nuns and villagers accept
her. I'm sure she can take over my duties
here, including our meetings with the
villagers."

After Teresa finishes reading the letter, she is
silent.

                    BEATRICE

    It's a very good letter. Thank you
for recommending me.

                    TERESA

    Do you feel it is complete?

                    BEATRICE

    What about your new calling? You
don't say anything about God's guidance
in your life.

                    TERESA

    You're right. I could add something
about being called in a different
direction by God.

                    BEATRICE

    Have you spoken to any of the other
sisters about this?

                    TERESA

    Only to you and Luisa. I must also
ask permission from the sisters to leave.

                    BEATRICE

    Not all the sisters at once! You
might open a Pandora's box of jealousies!

                    TERESA

You think so?

                    BEATRICE

May I make a suggestion?

                    TERESA

Of course.

                    BEATRICE

     You should speak to the Mother
Superior, if we had one. Sister Helen has
been here the longest, so she plays the
role of Mother Superior when necessary.

                    TERESA

I don't know her well.

                    BEATRICE

     She was not sympathetic to Luisa's
request. Maybe she will be more
compassionate toward you.

                                SUPERIMPOSITION
                                TO NEXT SCENE.

INT. CHAPEL. A WEEK LATER. MORNING.

Teresa genuflects at the entrance to the chapel, then
walks toward the altar where Sister Helen is seated.

                    TERESA

Sister Helen . . .

HELEN

You asked to see me, Sister Teresa.
Here I am.

TERESA

Thank you for agreeing to see me.

HELEN

You have not had a meeting with the
villagers in a month.

TERESA

You're right. I was in Toledo
visiting my widowed father, who asked to
see me.

HELEN

The constable brought us numerous
people to chastise this month, while you
were away.

TERESA

I'm sorry to hear it. Sister
Beatrice could have led the meetings in
my absence.

HELEN

You should have arranged it before
you left!

TERESA

Yes, but there is another matter I
wish to speak about with you.

HELEN

What is it?

TERESA

While I was in Toledo I happened to meet a painter at the Cathedral Church. He fell in love with me and proposed marriage. I would like to marry him.

HELEN

I see. You would like my permission to leave the convent.

TERESA

Yes. I would like to leave honorably, with your blessing.

HELEN

Have you spoken with your father about this?

TERESA

Yes! He's very happy about it and has given us his blessing! He has given me his villa so my husband and I can live there with him. It's a large villa.

Helen sighs heavily.

HELEN

You are asking a great deal, Teresa. The convent has not been the same this month.

TERESA

I have missed the sisters. But I miss my fiance much more.

HELEN

You were called to be a nun, to be a servant to our Lord Jesus Christ. You took a vow of loyalty and obedience to the Church.

Teresa straightens her shoulders and stands tall.

                    TERESA

     Now I believe I am called in a
different direction. I am called to be a
wife to Juan, and to be a householder and
farmer.

                    HELEN

     This is arrogance, and disobedience
to the vow you took to the Church! I
cannot give my approval.

                    TERESA

     Have you ever released a nun from
the convent?

                    HELEN

     That is an impertinent question.

                    TERESA

     I'm sorry.

                    HELEN

     You may have heard that there is
another sister who seeks to leave and
marry.

Teresa is silent.

                    HELEN (CONT'D)

     I have not given her permission to
leave, if you must know. I mention it
only because you probably have already
heard about it.

     We must try not to be selfish in
these matters, Teresa. You can do more
good for God and the world here in the
convent.

TERESA

Perhaps. But I can pray anywhere, and I can write about my experiences anywhere.

HELEN

Have you notified your confessor, the Inquisitor in Madrid?

TERESA

I've sent him a letter.

HELEN

It's too soon to expect a reply on such a serious matter. You will just have to wait.

Helen rises, heavily.

HELEN (CONT'D)

That is all I have to say today. I hope you will not be too disappointed.

Teresa is silent. Helen exits. Teresa kneels to pray.

SUPERIMPOSITION
TO NEXT SCENE.

EXT. YARD OUTSIDE CONVENT. A FEW DAYS LATER. AFTERNOON.

A group of villagers have gathered. Enter Teresa and Beatrice.

ELSA

Welcome back, Sister Teresa! You stayed away a whole month!

TERESA

Not quite a month. Three and a half weeks.

                    CARLOS

     There were no meetings while you
were away.

                    TERESA

     That was my mistake. Next time
Sister Beatrice will take my place and
lead the meetings.

A hush falls over the group.

                    BEATRICE

     Thank you, Sister Teresa. There has
been some trouble in the village this
month.

                    (MORE)

                BEATRICE (CONT'D)

     The constable brought us several
persons for confession.

                LADY GONZALEZ

What was the trouble?

                    BEATRICE

     Domestic disputes. Husbands and
wives who were squabbling and fighting.
But that is all in the past. We are here
to begin again.

                    TERESA

     We're glad to see you all again.
Welcome to our meeting! We will hold a
meeting like this every Wednesday. What
did you miss about our meetings?

MARITZA

I missed the chance to talk to someone besides my husband!

ELSA

I missed Sister Teresa's wise counsel.

LADY GONZALEZ

I also missed your counsel, Sister Teresa.

BEATRICE

What about the men?

CARLOS

I like to hear what other men are talking about.

LOPE

I learn something about myself from listening to the others.

CARLOS

It's good to know what other men do at home with their wives and children. Sometimes the women have more to say than the men do!

LOPE

That's certainly true.

A few people laugh.

BEATRICE

Today I've brought a story from the Holy Bible, something for us all to think about. I have written notes about this parable from the Bible, Matthew chapter 13. You have probably heard it in church services.

She reads from her notes.

                    BEATRICE (CONT'D)

     "A sower went forth to sow; and when
he sowed some seeds fell by the wayside,
and the birds gobbled them up. Some seeds
fell on stony places, where they had not
much earth; and they sprouted quickly.
When the sun came up, they were scorched;
and because they had no roots, they
withered away.

                    BEATRICE (CONT'D)

     "But other seeds fell into good
ground, and brought forth fruit, some a
hundredfold, some sixtyfold, some
thirtyfold."

                    BEATRICE (CONT'D)

     That is the parable of the sower.
What do you think it means?

The group is silent for a moment.

                    ELSA

     Are the seeds like the words of
Jesus?

                    BEATRICE

     Yes. That's a very good
observation, Elsa.

                    LADY GONZALEZ

     Then the ground is like the
listeners to the Word.

                    CARLOS

     I am like the wayside. The birds
ate my seed!

Some laugh at Carlos's remark.

TERESA

But you are here at our meeting, Carlos. The words spoken here have meant something to you.

CARLOS

Yes, sister. I was only joking.

LADY GONZALEZ

We should all try to be like the good soil and bring forth good actions.

TERESA

That's a very important point, Lady Gonzalez.

BEATRICE

I think it is the main point of the parable. You have summarized it well!

A pause for silence.

BEATRICE (CONT'D)

Any other comments on the parable?

Everyone is silent.

TERESA

You haven't met together for a month. Is there anything you want to ask or talk about?

MARITZA

I have something to discuss.

TERESA

Yes, Maritza?

MARITZA

Last week a neighbor came by to ask
me for flour to bake bread. I gave her a
whole basket of flour from the flour I
had brought from the market. But she
hasn't returned it!

CARLOS

Why don't you go to her house and
ask her for the flour?

MARITZA

Because she may not have enough
flour. That's why she came to me.

BEATRICE

Do you have enough money to buy more
flour from the market?

MARITZA

Just barely enough. I had to use
all the flour I had to make bread for my
family this week.

ELSA

If you have enough money to buy
flour, shouldn't you use the money?
Consider the flour you gave to your less
fortunate neighbor a gift.

MARITZA

I hope she doesn't ask again. I will have
to say no.

TERESA

You're right, Maritza. If you have
barely enough money to buy food for your
family, you cannot afford to give away
food to your neighbor.

It is a beautiful gesture to give a gift to a less fortunate neighbor. But your first responsibility is to take care of your husband and your own children.

INT. TERESA'S ROOM AT THE CONVENT. EVENING, SAME DAY.

Teresa reads a letter she has written to Juan. She tries to hold back tears.

TERESA

"Dearest Juan, I've been back at the convent only ten days, but it seems much longer since I last saw you. I miss you and think of you every day.

"The news here is not as I would wish. Sister Helen, who acts as our Mother Superior, has not released me from my vows as a nun in order to marry you. She says I am being selfish. She has also refused the request of Sister Luisa, a novice, who wishes to marry.

Teresa puts down her pen angrily. She walks to the window and looks out.

TERESA (V.O.)

"How sorry I am to tell you this news! I feel as if my future has been closed off, like a big black door has shut in my face. I've written to my Inquisitor, telling him I am called in another direction. No reply has come yet. It is too soon to expect anything from Madrid.

She returns to her desk, picks up her pen.

                    TERESA (CONT'D)

        "How is your painting progressing?
    I hope life goes well for you in Toledo,
    Juan. I'm grateful you have come into my
    life. Whatever happens, you have my
    deepest love and affection."

Teresa puts the letter in an addressed envelope and
seals it.

                              SUPERIMPOSITION
                              TO NEXT SCENE.

INT. CHAPEL. NEXT DAY. MORNING.

Sunlight streams in through the stained glass
windows. The nuns are seated for noon-time prayer.
Teresa is seated among them, looking miserable but
trying to hide her sadness.

The nuns stand to sing a hymn. Teresa stands too and,
as she begins to sing, her eyes fill with tears. She
stops singing. She does not rise above the ground.

INT. TERESA'S ROOM AT THE CONVENT. SAME DAY,
AFTERNOON.

Teresa writes in her journal, not bothering to hide
her sadness in the solitude of her room.

                              SUPERIMPOSITION
                              TO NEXT SCENE.

INT. HALLWAY ADJOINING THE CHAPEL. EVENING.

As the nuns file back into the chapel for evening
prayer, Teresa stops to look out of the window in the
hallway. She gazes at the moon, a slim crescent.

INT. CHAPEL. SAME DAY, EVENING.

The nuns are gathered for evening prayer. Teresa,
still looking sad, prays with the others.

Sister Helen is seated nearby. She notices Teresa and her misery.

The nuns stand to sing a hymn. Teresa stands but does not sing. She does not levitate. Sister Helen notices this too.

SUPERIMPOSITION
TO NEXT SCENE.

EXT. CONVENT YARD. A WEEK LATER.

Teresa greets the villagers who have gathered for their meeting.

TERESA

Welcome to you all. We're glad to see you here today. I am not feeling well so Sister Beatrice has agreed to lead the meeting.

Teresa sits among the villagers to listen.

BEATRICE

Thank you, Sister Teresa. We hope you will recover your good health and good spirits soon.

BEATRICE (CONT'D)

This week the constable brought us only one person for confession. I know you are curious about the nature of the offense. Let us say it was a domestic dispute.

SUPERIMPOSITION
TO NEXT SCENE.

INT. CHAPEL. SAME DAY. EVENING.

The nuns have gathered for evening prayer. Teresa appears numb with sadness.

Sister Helen looks at Teresa, hoping to see her spirit renewed. She sees that Teresa is still suffering.

The nuns start to sing. Teresa stands with them but doesn't sing or levitate.

SUPERIMPOSITION
TO NEXT SCENE.

INT. CONVENT ENTRANCE. A WEEK LATER. AFTERNOON.

A knock at the door. Sister Luisa opens it. Juan is in the doorway.

> LUISA
>
> Good afternoon, sir. What can we do for you?

> JUAN
>
> I would like to see Sister Teresa.

> LUISA
>
> She will be here soon. We have finished the noontime prayer.

For a moment, the screen is filled with nuns in black habits coming out of the chapel. Teresa is among them. She sees Juan and leaves the group, walks quickly to embrace him.

> TERESA
>
> Juan, what a wonderful surprise! I can't believe you're here!

> JUAN
>
> As soon as I received your letter, I made arrangements to visit. I had to see you!

                    TERESA

          Where will you stay?

                    JUAN

          I have an idea. Perhaps Sister
     Helen would like a painting.

                    TERESA

          That's a very good idea! But do you
     have time to paint a commission here?

                    JUAN

          I   have   permission   from   Father
     Francisco. My master is staying in Rome
     awhile longer so I will not be missed.

                    TERESA

          Luisa, would you ask Sister Helen
     to speak with our visitor?

                    LUISA

          Certainly.

          Luisa exits, looking for Sister
     Helen among the nuns.

                    JUAN

          Can't we have some time together?

                    TERESA

          After you've been introduced. I
     don't want Sister Helen to think I am
     seeing you in secret, behind her back.

     Juan kisses her hand.

                    JUAN

          I'm so grateful to see you again.

Enter Sister Luisa and Sister Helen.

                    TERESA

        Sister Helen, this is my fiance,
    Juan Calder.

                    HELEN

        Hello, sir. You know you cannot
    have a visitor stay at the convent,
    Teresa.

Before Teresa can reply, Juan speaks up.

                    JUAN

        Sister Helen, would you like to
    have a new painting?

                    HELEN

        Thank you for your offer, but we
    have no money for paintings.

                    JUAN

        It is a gift, a present from the
    Cathedral Church of Toledo.

                    (MORE)

                JUAN (CONT'D)

        You don't have to pay a thing. I
    brought all my supplies with me.

Sister Helen's feathers are smoothed by Juan's good
manners as well as his offer.

                    HELEN

        Well, I suppose we could use
    another painting.

JUAN

     An image of our Lord? Or of the
Virgin Mary? Perhaps you could sit for a
portrait of Mary.

                HELEN

     Don't be foolish. Nobody wants to
look at an old woman. But you could give
her Teresa's face.

                JUAN

     As you wish.

                HELEN

     We will have to find a place for
you to stay. Perhaps the caretaker will
let you have his extra room while you
paint.

                JUAN

     Thank you. You are generous.

                TERESA

     Where will you paint?

                JUAN

     I can paint anywhere. Even
outdoors, as long as there is no rain.

                HELEN

     Teresa, you may show him the
convent yard. He can make the painting
there. I hope this will lift your
spirits.

Teresa nods obediently and leads Juan to the yard.

                TERESA

     Come with me, Juan.

EXT. CONVENT YARD. A FEW MINUTES LATER.

Teresa and Juan come out of the convent into the yard.

                    JUAN

        Now can we have some time alone?

                    TERESA

        Yes, but somebody may come at any
moment. We are never really alone here.

                    JUAN

        I'm happy I have permission to
paint you. I thought she would want a
portrait of our Lord Jesus.

                    TERESA

        It will give us a reason to spend
time together. Have you ever painted the
Virgin Mary before?

                    JUAN

        As part of a group of figures. We
worked on a canvas of the Holy Family.
But this will be my first portrait of the
Virgin alone. You will be a beautiful
Mary.

                    TERESA

        You flatter me, Juan.

                    JUAN

        Even Sister Helen seems to think
so! I'm so happy to see you again. Have
you had a reply from Madrid yet?

                    TERESA

        Nothing yet.

                         JUAN

          Perhaps it's a good sign. At least
     they have not said "no."

                        TERESA

     You're right. It may be a good sign.

Juan kisses her. As Teresa responds, Sister Luisa
enters. Juan and Teresa end the kiss.

                        LUISA

          Pardon me. Sister Helen wants to
     speak to you, Juan.

Juan and Teresa stand apart.

Enter Sister Helen. Sister Luisa exits.

                        HELEN

          I have found a place for the painting. In
     the chapel! Would you like to see it?

                         JUAN

     Yes, indeed.

                        HELEN

     You may come along, Sister Teresa.

Sister Helen exits, followed by Juan and Teresa.

INT. CHAPEL. A FEW MINUTES LATER.

Sister Helen, Juan and Teresa have entered the
chapel.

                        HELEN

          This area here, next to the High
     Altar, seems a bit empty. I think your
     painting could be placed here.

                    JUAN

     I see what you mean. The crucifix
is at the center.

                    HELEN

     Yes, and the Virgin Mary would be next to
him.

                    JUAN

     Very well. This is helpful, to see
the setting and the surrounding artwork,
including the crucifix of course.

                    HELEN

     Yes!

                    JUAN

     It's a lovely chapel, Sister Helen.
I shall be honored to have a painting
hanging here.

                    HELEN

     Well, what are we waiting for? Are
you ready to start working?

                    JUAN

     Yes! I'll stretch the canvas today.
I think I have a frame that is the right
size for the space.

                    HELEN

     Good. I'll tell the caretaker that
he will have a guest. How long will you
need to make the painting?

                    JUAN

Normally we need a month or two.

                    HELEN

     A month is a long time to house a
guest.

Juan thinks for a moment.

                    JUAN

     Maybe I can complete it in two
weeks.

                    HELEN

     All right. Two weeks.

                              SUPERIMPOSITION
                                TO NEXT SCENE.

EXT. CONVENT YARD. EARLY EVENING.

Juan completes the task of stretching the canvas onto
the frame. He begins painting the canvas with beige
paint.

Enter Teresa carrying supper. She places the tray on
a table.

                    TERESA

     This is our humble supper, Juan.
The bread is very good.

                    JUAN

     Will you dine with me?

                    TERESA

     Yes, I brought my supper too.

                    JUAN

     It's getting cooler. Take my coat.

Juan removes his coat and wraps it around her
shoulders tenderly.

Juan has put down his paintbrush. He covers the painting, then draws up two chairs to the table. He and Teresa sit down to dinner together.

                         TERESA

        Gracious God, we thank you for this
     meal. Thank you for bringing Juan here to
     visit. This is a very special gift. Amen.

                         JUAN

        Amen.

Juan kisses her hand. They eat supper.

                              SUPERIMPOSITION
                              TO NEXT SCENE.

EXT. CONVENT YARD. NEXT DAY AFTERNOON.

The canvas is on Juan's easel. The composition is sketched onto the beige background. Juan is painting the larger areas -- the white dress of the Virgin, the dark areas of the background.

                              SUPERIMPOSITION
                              TO NEXT SCENE.

EXT. CONVENT YARD. A FEW DAYS LATER. MORNING.

Teresa is posing in her white undergarment as Juan paints her as the Virgin Mary. Enter Sister Helen.

                         HELEN

        How is the painting progressing,
     Juan?

                         JUAN

        Very well, I think.

HELEN

Teresa, what are you doing without your robe?

TERESA

Juan says the black cloak makes the painting too dark.

JUAN

To portray the Virgin Mary in a black robe will make a very dark painting. I would like Mary to be glowing with light. That corner of the chapel would benefit from light colors.

HELEN

I understand. But we will have trouble if the other nuns see Teresa standing here in her undergarment.

JUAN

Do you have a colorful robe we could borrow? I can use my imagination but it's better if I can see my model in an appropriate color.

HELEN

Let me see. We have robes in red, purple, we have one robe in blue . . .

JUAN

Blue would be perfect! The Virgin is often painted in a blue robe.

HELEN

Very well. I will get the robe for you, Teresa.

TERESA

Thank you, Sister Helen.

After Helen exits, Teresa and Juan have a laugh
together.

SUPERIMPOSITION
TO NEXT SCENE.

EXT. CONVENT YARD. NEXT DAY. AFTERNOON.

Teresa poses in the blue robe. Juan is painting the
blue robe. The face of the Virgin Mary is suggested
but not yet fully realized.

SUPERIMPOSITION
TO NEXT SCENE.

EXT. CONVENT YARD. TWO DAYS LATER. EARLY AFTERNOON.

Closeup on Teresa's face, then a closeup of Mary's
face in the painting. Juan is completing the face in
the painting.

SUPERIMPOSITION
TO NEXT SCENE.

EXT. TABLE IN CONVENT YARD. SAME DAY, EVENING.

Juan and Teresa sit at dinner together. The figure
and face of the Virgin Mary are painted on the canvas,
sitting on Juan's easel.

                    JUAN

    Do you like the painting, Teresa?

                    TERESA

    Yes, very much. You have idealized
    my face and form.

                    JUAN

    No, you are perfect as you are.

98

                    TERESA

     What   will   you   do   with   the
background?

                    JUAN

     I'm thinking about it. I painted
you -- as Mary -- so quickly that I may
finish early. I might have to add some
objects to the background to fill in the
time.

                    TERESA

     Add some objects! Don't finish
early. Leave some of the painting
unfinished. That way maybe Helen will
want you to stay longer.

Juan smiles.

                    JUAN

     This   is   exactly   what   I   was
thinking.

                    TERESA

     Be sure to cover the painting! I
don't want the others to see how quickly
it's progressing.

Juan rises and covers the painting carefully with a
large dropcloth.

                              SUPERIMPOSITION
                              TO NEXT SCENE.

EXT. CONVENT YARD. NEXT DAY, AFTERNOON.

Juan has set a bowl of fruit and a chalice on the
table. He is adding these objects into the background
of the painting. Teresa watches, contented to be in
Juan's presence as he works.

Enter Sister Luisa with a letter on a tray. Sister Jana follows.

                         JANA

    Your portrait is almost finished, Teresa!

                        TERESA

    The background is not finished yet.

                         JANA

    What will you do when Juan has to leave? Will you go back to being sad and miserable?

                         JUAN

    I am not done with the painting yet. I'm not leaving until the painting is finished.

                        LUISA

    Sister Teresa . . .

Luisa shows Teresa the letter.

                        TERESA

    It's from the Inquisition!

Juan reacts, subtly.

                        LUISA

    Come, Sister Jana, let's give them some privacy.

                         JANA

    What's in the letter?

                        LUISA

    Come now, Jana. This is none of your business.

Jana exits reluctantly, grumbling. Sister Luisa follows.

                    JANA

          None   of   my   business!   The
     Inquisition is everybody's business!

Teresa and Juan look at each other.

                    TERESA

          You open it, Juan.

Juan looks at the letter.

                    JUAN

          The letter is addressed to you. You
     should open it.

With trembling fingers, Teresa opens the letter and
reads it silently.

                    JUAN (CONT'D)

          What does it say?

                    TERESA

          It says I must go to Madrid to speak
     with the Inquisitor.

She shows him the letter.

                    JUAN

          It doesn't say "no." This may be a
     good sign.

                    TERESA

          Maybe you're right!

                    JUAN

          You can ride in my wagon with me to
     Madrid.

                    TERESA

      Will you drive there with me, Juan?

                    JUAN

      Yes. I want to know what happens!

Sister Helen enters.

                    TERESA

      Hello, Sister Helen.

                    HELEN

      Good   afternoon,   Teresa.   Good
      afternoon, Juan. I see the painting is
      coming along well.

                    JUAN

      Thank you. I hope you'll be pleased
      with the result.

                    HELEN

      Teresa, I understand you have a
      letter from the Inquisitor in Madrid.

Teresa shows her the letter.

                    TERESA

      I am summoned to Madrid next week.

                    HELEN

      This will be an important meeting
      for your future.

                    TERESA

      Yes.

                    HELEN

      It will be important for all of us.
      I will tell the caretaker to make ready

the carriage for you to use on your
journey.

                    JUAN

     Sister Helen, I would like to take
Sister Teresa to Madrid in my wagon. I
will be done with the painting by next
week.

                   HELEN

     All right, Juan. This meeting will
change your life, one way or another!

                    JUAN

     Yes.

                   HELEN

     Your presence has been a good
influence. You've lifted Teresa's
spirits -- and we have a beautiful new
painting of the blessed Virgin!

                    JUAN

     I'm pleased that you like the
painting.

                   HELEN

     Now back to work! You must finish
the painting.

                    JUAN

     Yes, Sister Helen.

Juan returns to painting. Sister Helen exits. Teresa
reads the letter again, silently.

                              SUPERIMPOSITION
                              TO NEXT SCENE.

.

INT. CHAPEL. A FEW DAYS LATER. AFTERNOON.

Juan is hanging the new painting in the chapel. Sister Helen and Sister Teresa watch.

                    HELEN

     The painting glows with light! You were right to insist on the blue robe.

                    JUAN

     Yes!

                    HELEN

     Now I understand. The painting illuminates this dark corner of the chapel. Thank you, Juan.

                    JUAN

     You are most welcome, Sister Helen. I'm glad you're pleased. Father Francisco in Toledo will be glad to hear it.

                    HELEN

     And now we have a portrait of Sister Teresa to keep with us.

                    (MORE)

              HELEN (CONT'D)

     Whatever happens in Madrid, you will always be here with us in the painting, Teresa.

Sister Helen touches Teresa tenderly, a rare touch from Helen.

                    TERESA

     Thank you, Sister Helen.

                    HELEN

     Now you must make ready for your
trip to Madrid.

                   TERESA

     I'm ready, Sister Helen.

                              SUPERIMPOSITION
                              TO NEXT SCENE.

EXT. CONVENT ENTRANCE. TWO DAYS LATER. MORNING.

In the background, Juan waits with his horse and
wagon. In foreground, Teresa says good-bye to Sister
Helen, Sister Beatrice and Sister Luisa.

                   TERESA

     Good-bye, Sister Helen. I hope the
meetings with the villagers go well.

                  BEATRICE

     I'll do my best to lead the
discussion.

                    HELEN

     It's good that you have made
arrangements to continue the meetings in
Teresa's absence.

                   TERESA

     Sister Luisa, I have not forgotten
my promise to you.

                   LUISA

     Thank you, Sister Teresa.

                    HELEN

     So we may lose two of our best
sisters to the world.

TERESA

You still have Sister Beatrice! I
must go now. I should not keep Juan
waiting.

HELEN

Good-bye then. Have a safe journey!

LUISA

Safe travels, Teresa!

Teresa goes to Juan's wagon. He helps her up into the
wagon and kisses her hand. They wave good-bye to the
sisters and depart.

SUPERIMPOSITION
TO NEXT SCENE.

INT. CATHEDRAL IN MADRID. TWO DAYS LATER. AFTERNOON.

FATHER RUIZ stands near the altar. Teresa enters at
the back of the nave and genuflects.

FATHER RUIZ

You arrived quickly! Come forward.

She gets up and walks toward him.

TERESA

I received permission to travel as
soon as I was summoned.

FATHER RUIZ

We have read your letter.

TERESA

Father Ruiz, I recognize this is a
serious question. I hope I have not
jeopardized my family.

FATHER RUIZ

We release women – and men – from their vows to the Church when they are called to the life of a householder.

TERESA

I know I am not the first to break my vows.

FATHER RUIZ

You did not break your vow. You have been called in a different direction.

TERESA

Yes.

FATHER RUIZ

Do you feel the hand of God in all this?

TERESA

(speaking thoughtfully)

I care for Juan more than . . .

FATHER RUIZ

Juan is the name of your fiancé?

TERESA

Yes! I care more for him than I imagined I could care for anybody, even my parents. I feel nothing but love and light and kindness between us.

FATHER RUIZ

I feel the hand of God here. I think you feel His presence as well.

TERESA nods in assent. The priest smiles warmly, surprising even himself with his warmth of feeling.

                    FATHER RUIZ (CONT'D)

          You have my blessing, Teresa. I am
     so happy I can scarcely contain myself!

He chuckles, bubbling over with joy, then stops himself when he sees Teresa is puzzled.

               Please do not be sad. We shall miss
          your presence in our mission. Would you
          prefer to see me weep?

                    TERESA

          Of course not.

                    FATHER RUIZ

               I am as surprised as you are! I did
          not want to scold you but I did not expect
          to feel such delight about your future!

A moment of silent communion.

                    TERESA

               I have thought carefully and asked
          for God's guidance. The villagers want to
          continue our weekly meetings, and our
          Mother Superior has given her approval.

                    FATHER RUIZ

               Have you found a successor, someone
          to lead the meetings?

                    TERESA

               I would choose from among the
          sisters at the convent.

                    FATHER RUIZ

          Good.

TERESA

I would suggest Sister Beatrice. She leads the meetings in my absence. The villagers seem to accept her as their leader.

FATHER RUIZ

Very good.

TERESA

There is one more matter concerning another sister at the convent.

FATHER RUIZ

Yes?

TERESA

A novice has fallen in love with one of the villagers, a prominent citizen. He wishes to marry her.

FATHER RUIZ

I see.

TERESA

I told her I would plead her case to you.

FATHER RUIZ

It seems at least one of your sisters wishes to follow your example, Teresa.

TERESA

I hope I have not been a bad influence. The prospective fiancé is Senor Mariposa.

                    FATHER RUIZ

     Mariposa? I know the name.

                    TERESA

     He is a proud man, not popular with
the villagers. He was deeply disappointed
when one of the village girls rejected
his proposal of marriage.

                    FATHER RUIZ

     You knew about her refusal?

                    TERESA

     He told me, Father. The girl's
family asked for my help and protection.
The girl did not like Senor Mariposa at
all. She was frightened by him.

                    FATHER RUIZ

     What did you think of him?

                    TERESA

     I was frightened by him too,
frightened by his anger.

                    FATHER RUIZ

     I understand. Now he has found a
young lady who likes him, but she happens
to be one of your nuns.

                    TERESA

     Yes, Father.

                    FATHER RUIZ

     We shall release her from her vows
as well, and hope she can tame this
hurricane named Mariposa.

                      TERESA

     Thank you, Father. The entire
village would join in thanking you, if
they knew.

             FATHER RUIZ

     Are there any other nuns with
similar requests?

                   TERESA

     No, Father. As far as I know, the
other nuns are content to serve the
Church.

                 FATHER RUIZ

     Thank you for coming promptly to
see us, Teresa. I shall miss our
conversations.

                   TERESA

          (surprised) Thank you, Father.

     He blesses her and she departs.

EXT. STREET OUTSIDE MADRID CATHEDRAL. CONTINUOUS.

Juan is waiting for Teresa with his horse and
carriage. Teresa walks out of the cathedral.

                    JUAN

        Teresa!

She embraces and kisses him, overjoyed.

                    JUAN (CONT'D)

What happened?

                    TERESA

I am released from my vows to the
sisterhood! The Inquisitor has given me
his blessing!

                    JUAN

That's wonderful! I'm so happy!

He picks her up and twirls her around.

Now we don't need Sister Helen's
approval, do we?

                    TERESA

No, but she will approve since the
Inquisitor approves.

                    JUAN

Now can you come home to Toledo?

                    TERESA

Yes, I can. Toledo will be my new
home.

Juan embraces her passionately.

                    JUAN

I cannot believe this day has
arrived! I could not be happier!

                    TERESA

Don't forget Sister Luisa.

                    JUAN

The other nun who wants to marry?

                    TERESA

     Yes. She is released from her vows
to the Church as well.

                    JUAN

     Would you like to see her and the
sisters again?

                    TERESA

     Yes! Would you come with me again
to Avila?

                    JUAN

     I could not bear to let you go
alone.

Sister Luisa enters from the shadows.

                    TERESA

     Luisa! I didn't know that you're
here!

                    LUISA

     Pepe insisted. He couldn't wait for
the news to come back to Avila.

In the shadows, we recognize Senor Mariposa. He
greets them all.

                    MARIPOSA

     Greetings,   Sister   Teresa.
Greetings, Senor. Thank you for helping
LUISA to be released from her vows!

                    LUISA

     I'm only a novice. It's not the same
as being released from a nun's vows.

TERESA

All the same, it's a big change and a new calling. I wish you both happiness and peace.

MARIPOSA

Thank you. Come now, LUISA, the carriage is waiting.

LUISA

Farewell, Sister Teresa. I hope we'll meet again!

Senor Mariposa escorts LUISA to the waiting carriage.

FADEOUT

EXT. CONVENT YARD IN AVILA. A FEW WEEKS LATER, AFTERNOON.

Villagers, Teresa and Juan, Senor Mariposa and LUISA dance a simple partner dance. Guitar music accompanies the dance. The nuns watch the dancing and listen to the music with delight.

---end of screenplay---

PUBLIC READING presented October 29, 2013, 3:15 pm, at Frederick Loewe Room, Dramatists Guild of America, New York, NY. Producer: Z.R.D., Inc. (Earlier draft of the script.)

DEAR SISTER TERESA
Fictional historical drama
by Amy L. Heebner

PREFACE:
ACTOR - Stephen Diacrussi*
WRITER - Amy Heebner
NARRATOR - Amy Heebner

MADRID CATHEDRAL:
INQUISITOR - Fred Bender
TERESA - Maite Uzal*

AVILA:
TERESA - Maite Uzal*
BEATRICE - Amy Heebner
LADY GONZALEZ - Zana Markelson
LOPE, war veteran
SENOR MARIPOSA

TOLEDO:
JUAN - Stephen Diacrussi*
ALONSO, Teresa's father- Fred Bender
MIRA, Teresa's sister- Amy Heebner

*Actor appears courtesy of Actors Equity Association, U.S.A.
Understudies: Roy James Brown, Amy Heebner (for Teresa), Tameran Josbeck, Christina Korteweg.
Audition Assistant: Christina Korteweg.
Director: Amy Heebner.
On October 29, 2013, the roles of Lope and Mariposa were read by Fred Bender and Stephen Diacrussi.*

ACKNOWLEDGEMENTS

SPECIAL THANKS to the cast of actors and actresses; to the Dramatists Guild of America and Friday Night Footlights for support with presentation space; to Ruedi and my family for their support and encouragement; to the Writers Guild of America, East; to the hundreds of actors and actresses who expressed interest in this and other projects; to BACKSTAGE magazine.

ABOUT THE WRITER

Amy Heebner is a screenwriter, playwright and scholar who resides in New York City. Her first screenplay, Missing Data, achieved Finalist status in the New Century Writer screenplay competition. She received a private grant for writing.Dr. Heebner has worked in theater and post-secondary education in the U.S. and Switzerland. She has also worked as a visual artist and videographer.

She owes a special kind of gratitude to her parents and her late Swiss husband, Ruedi Kaegi, for their support and encouragement.

Dr. Heebner is a member of the Dramatists Guild of America. Feel free to send questions and constructive comments to her by e-mail at zinniares@aol.com. More Information may be found at www.amyheebnerwriting.com